C. W Hall

The University of Minnesota

An historical sketch

C. W Hall

The University of Minnesota
An historical sketch

ISBN/EAN: 9783337036492

Printed in Europe, USA, Canada, Australia, Japan

Cover: Foto ©ninafisch / pixelio.de

More available books at **www.hansebooks.com**

THE

University of Minnesota

AN HISTORICAL SKETCH

BY

DEAN C. W. HALL

MINNEAPOLIS
1896

An Historical Sketch.

By C. W. HALL.

(This sketch was prepared for the GOPHER of the Class of '97 and through the courtesy of the Editors this separate print is issued.)

EXTERNAL EVENTS--Early Incidents.

On February 25, 1851, the Governor of the Territory of Minnesota, Alexander Ramsey, approved an act of incorporation by which the University of the Territory of Minnesota began its legal existence. The same act located the institution at or near the Falls of Saint Anthony. That tells substantially the whole story of its first year, for at the first meeting of the Board of Regents designated in the act—Messrs. Henry H. Sibley, Franklin Steele, Alexander Ramsey, Isaac Atwater, B. B. Meeker, Socrates Nelson, C. K. Smith, William R. Marshall, N. C. D. Taylor, Henry M. Rice, Abraham Van Vorches, John H. Stevens and G. J. Y. Rhieldaffer—held the third day of June following, in the city of Saint Anthony, nothing but a situation confronted them. There was no endowment, no money,

The Original University Building, Architect's Ideal, 1856.

had been appropriated, and the work of the Board consisted in talk—talking over the location of the new institution, the raising of means for its support, arousing the interest of citizens and suggesting anything and everything to ensure the success of the new enterprise. Following this meeting came the first gift to education which Minnesota had received. It was the gift of Regent Steele, formally tendered to the Regents in 1852, of a site on which to build the University. Means were obtained for erecting a building upon this ground, now occupied by the Exposition building of Minneapolis. Under the principalship of Rev. E. W. Merrill, in November 1851, the preliminary school of the University was opened to students. For three years and a half, with an average attendance of sixty scholars, Mr. Merrill prosecuted his work. By the end of this time it was seen that Franklin Steele's gift was inadequate to meet even the immediate needs of the University. As the Regents looked forward and calculated the growth of a quarter of a century they saw that more ground must be secured. The city of

Saint Anthony was growing; hence it should be secured at once. Accordingly, with money that had been obtained from the sale of certain lands, they purchased twenty-seven acres of the present campus. This selection of a site was in 1854. The sum of $6,000 was paid for the same, an amount which was large at that time. Until 1856 the new territory was prosperous even beyond the expectation of the most sanguine settlers, who had come here from New England to establish their homes in a territory declared by the government's exploring officers of the '30s to be uninhabitable, save for Indians and herds, and to be unproductive except for a few of the hardiest cereal crops.

The Original University Building as It Exists Today.

Accordingly, in 1856, there was begun upon the campus the erection of the University building. The plans for this building, as outlined by the architect duly appointed by the Regents, would do credit to the most sanguine millionaire in founding the University of today. The structure was to consist of a main part of four stories over a high basement, and two wings, each of three stories, over a high basement, the whole to be 277 feet in length Deciding at first to erect only a part of the magnificent structure proposed, the Regents, with the few thousand dollars then on hand, entered upon their work. They were urged to do it both by their own large views of what the territory was to become and by the clamors of people who were not disposed to see funds lying in the territorial treasury unused at a time full of such large needs for expenditure and grand opportunities for growth. The work of construction began; so too did those financial movements which resulted in disaster and ruin not only to the enterprise so auspiciously begun, but to the fortunes and prospects of some of the Regents themselves and many steadfast friends of the University. In the wild and unreasonable effort of distress to place blame at some responsible door, the Regents were charged not only with lack of judgment but even with a criminal misappropriation of public funds. An investigation was demanded and made. Its result was the full exoneration of the Board.

In all these troublous times the Regents never lost sight of the purposes of the University. In the spring of 1858 a second attempt to open the institution was made. Mr. Barber, a competent instructor, was employed to take charge of the preparatory department. At the expiration of six months the school was discontinued because the attendance was so small that tuitions would not half meet the expenses.

In 1860 the institution by legislative enactment was entirely reorganized and placed under a new Board of Regents—Alexander Ramsey, President; William R. Marshall, Edward D. Neill, Jared Benson, John M. Berry, Edward O. Hamilton, Uriah Thomas and William M. Kimball. But the state was not ready to take up educational work; the War of the Rebellion and the Sioux Indian outbreak held in abeyance all considerations beyond those of immediate necessity. A heavy debt had accumulated; the rate of interest in those days was from 12 to 24 per cent.; with no resources save lands which could not be sold, the situation was daily more alarming.

It was more than seven years before Minnesota, which meanwhile had become a state, felt ready again to resume the work of developing higher education. In the stress of events incident to the financial crash of 1857 followed by the War of the Rebellion and the Indian outbreak, the endowment of land made to the territory had been swept away and the appropriation due to Minnesota under the Morrill Act of 1862 was in jeopardy.

In 1864 a commission was created by the Legislature. This enactment was an act of salvation. John S. Pillsbury, John M. Nicols and Orlando C. Merriman were appointed to sell lands and pay debts until the last dollar had been met. Their work was not accomplished before 1867, in which year the situation was so promising that the Legislature appropriated money for the renovation of the long unused building.

Something had been saved, and on March 9, 1867, the Legislature voted its first cash appropriation for higher education—$15,000, to repair and furnish the University building, which since the 50's had stood unoccupied and crumbling. In October of that year Principal W. W. Washburn and two assistants began teaching. These assistants were Gabriel Campbell and Ira Moore. A goodly number of students, chiefly from the families in the neighborhood of the University, enrolled themselves in the new school. The work of this preparatory department was carried on for two years with such eminent success and satisfaction that it was felt by the Regents that the time had come to enlarge the field of instruction and correspondingly to increase the teaching force.

Among the perplexities of the Regents in early days some of the most annoying were associated with their efforts to maintain their charge as an educational institution. For instance, it was through the shrewd movements and decisive vote of one man that the state was once spared the conversion of the institution into an asylum for the insane.

Another question had to be answered at this point in the history of the institution, viz., whether co-education should be allowed. The Faculty brought the traditions of American colleges to bear. The Regents representing the Commonwealth voted the spirit of the Constitution into the University, and since that date the question of sex has never been raised except in the debating societies.

The decision, which appears to have been reached before President Folwell's arrival, was ably supported by him in the following inaugural words: "The University . . . exists for the benefit of society, not merely for that of individuals. Whether male or female, . . . the doors of its auditoria, its laboratories, its library stand open to all worthy comers; that is, to all persons of good fame, who prove themselves competent to hear and receive its lessons."

Both before and some time after this point in its history the University had been hampered by political influences; these influences grew up because there was money to be expended. Everywhere that such a condition exists, the politician is on hand and the early days in the history of the University of Minnesota are no exception to universal experience. But the Regents stood firm in their convictions that education should not be hampered by political or selfish desires. The constitution had already declared it free of sectarianism or other religious interference, and it remained with the Board further to insist upon perfect freedom from political intrigue. In this position they were supported by the educated men of the state and those were, for a young commonwealth, many and strong. So well did the Regents succeed in maintaining their position that no influence of this kind has for years been seen. A proposition practiced by Governor Pillsbury that no man should be appointed to an office of responsibility and trust in the State's affairs who had not proved his fitness therefor by the successful management of his own personal affairs, has been felt in the Capitol since Governor Pillsbury's six years' service as chief executive.

A serious difficulty confronting the Regents was that of starting aright in entering upon their work of founding a university. The first necessity of such an enterprise was the selection for the presidency of a man of courage, persistency, caution, bright scholarship and a large view of the future. It was essential that such a man be found to serve as pilot and guide in holding the institution to a steady policy of intellectual progress. The first duty of a president thus chosen is to mark out a reasonable and fair policy, and direct the energies of the administration to its proper and legitimate enforcement. In viewing the history of educational movements it is seen that all reforms have begun in the higher fields—those of knowledge and research—and thence, like rays of light, have penetrated downwards through the great mass of human society, until the plane of the every-day interests of life has become illumined. The condition requisite of success in an educational movement is that it be adapted to the conceptions and judgment of the people to be educated. Another is that it be pushed only at such speed that the community may keep pace understandingly, without chafing and unrest. The man for such a work was found in President Folwell, and the policy upon which he settled after months of careful study and consultation with some of the foremost educators in the country, was published in its general features as the action of the Regents in the early reports of the Board.

The Growth of the Campus.

It is not necessary to describe again the gift of Franklin Steele to the University. March 3d, 1854, the Regents decided to purchase a lot of land owned by Messrs. George and Taylor and thereon locate the new university. That lot comprised twenty-seven acres of the present Campus. It reached from the bank of the river to University avenue, but unfortunately extended along University avenue less than twelve rods. The price paid for this was $6,000. On the inauguration of plans for building in the early 70's, it was seen that a greater frontage was essential. Governor Pillsbury purchased by his own means the thousand feet along University avenue platted as Thatcher's Addition, and held it until the State could appropriate funds to reimburse him. This was done in February, 1877 and the most essential part of the Campus, a beautiful frontage, was secured from Twelfth avenue to Seventeenth, at an expense of $18,000. Soon, even this enlargement was found to be insufficient for the prospective needs of the immediate future. Again, the phenomenal growth of the cities, Minneapolis and Saint Paul, warned the Regents that what was done must be done quickly. Another appropriation for enlarging the Campus was asked and granted March 10, 1879, of $20,000. The next request for more ground was received by the legislature and approved in voting February 24, 1884, the sum of $20,000 in addition to the ordinary University budget. The final addition to the grounds

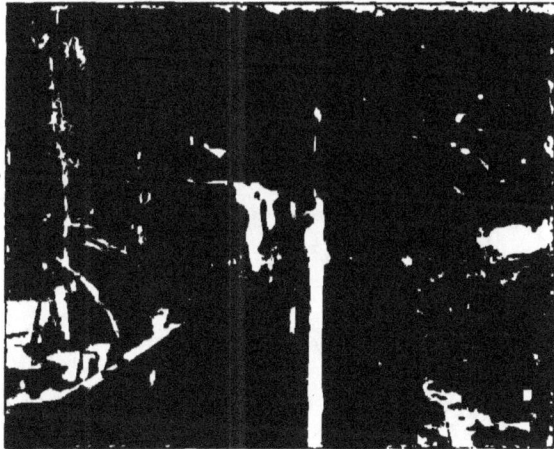

The Greenhouses.

The Plant House.

was made two years ago by the gift of the late Hon. Richard Chute, who had served for some years and at two different times as a Regent. The gift consists of a narrow strip extending on the south side of University avenue from Eleventh avenue southeast eastward. It has given that finish to the westward extension of the grounds, possible only when a street frontage is secured.

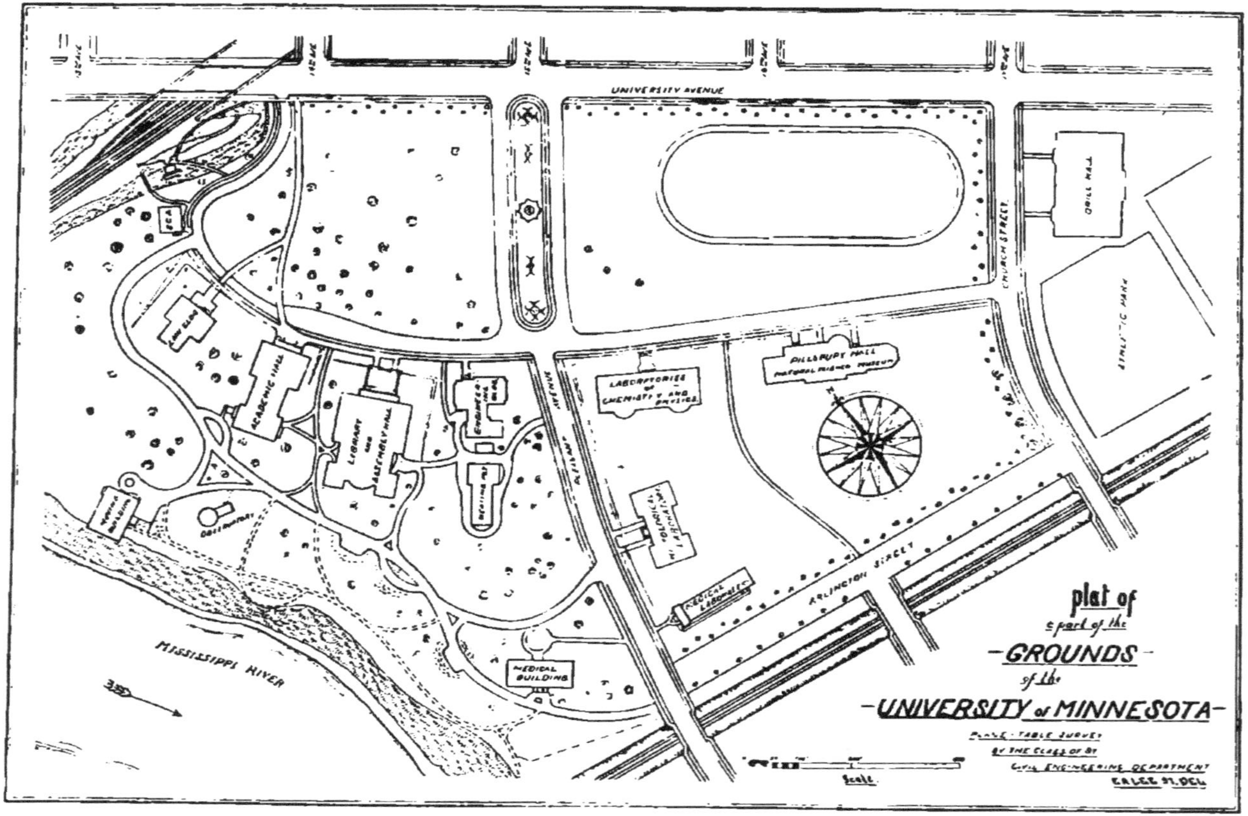

plat of
a part of the
-GROUNDS-
of the
-UNIVERSITY of MINNESOTA-
UNIVERSITY AVENUE
CHURCH STREET
ARLINGTON STREET
DRILL HALL
PILLSBURY HALL
LABORATORIES OF CHEMISTRY AND PHYSICS
MEDICAL BUILDING
ACADEMIC HALL
LIBRARY AND ASSEMBLY HALL
LAW BLDG
OBSERVATORY
MISSISSIPPI RIVER
Scale

Save in the erection upon it of the buildings, this piece of ground remained almost as nature left it until 1894. In that year the grounds were laid out by a distinguished landscape gardener and the legislature appropriated $12,500 the following winter for their improvement. Accordingly driveways have been opened,

A Touchdown.

stone sidewalks have been laid, the surface has been graded, and a well-planned system of improvements has been begun. Representing a total cost to the state of less than $80,000, it stands at current prices for several times that amount. It was planned in the 80's to make the Campus a grand Arboretum in which to grow every tree and shrub that would thrive in the state. The project was, for practical reasons, given up almost before any work and experimentation in that direction had been instituted. After the decision to open teaching colleges of law and medicine, it was soon realized that this ground would be needed for the rapidly developing lecture-room and laboratory work of the institution. The group of buildings which has sprung up as by magic, even now proves the wisdom of the step then taken.

The Campus, enlarged by these several increments, contains fifty acres. It is of magnificent extent and surpassingly beautiful in situation for a seat of learning. It stands in the very heart of a flourishing commercial and business center.

The Agricultural College Farm.

In accordance with the requirements of the act of reorganization, the Regents in 1868 purchased the Agricultural College Farm, a quarter of a mile east of the original University Campus. All preliminary arrangements were made and

The Barn.

the Regents announced that "so soon as the farmers send us a sufficient number of their sons," this department of the institution would be in a flourishing condition. Many lines of experimentation were entered upon during the subsequent years. Between 1875 and 1880 great activity was shown by Professor Lacy.

Recognizing the unfavorable conditions as to soil and drainage, he early advised removal to a more favorable locality.

Such removal was not effected in his day. When his successor, Professor Edward D. Porter, came, in 1881 and had devoted a year to investigation, he recommended that the farm be sold and a new one with good soil be purchased; that the Campus be utilized as an illustrative Arboretum and horticultural grounds; that farmers' lecture courses be pushed to every community in the state and other important lines of work be organized and operated. While Professor Porter's tireless energy was felt in every line of work within the College, his special ambition was to organize and develop "a First Class Experiment Station." And of such, indeed, he succeeded in laying the foundations. Upon this foundation one of the best and most successful experimental farms and experimental stations in the country has been built up.

A Farmhouse.

The Regents obtained authority from the legislature, in 1881, and sold the

The General Museum—Geology and Mineralogy.

farm by platting it into two hundred and eighty-one lots as the Regents' Addition to Minneapolis, and auctioning the same at public sale. About $150,000 was thus realized from an original investment of $8,000 and some lots are still on hand. The sale of the Minnetonka fruit farm authorized by the legislature of 1889, has made possible still other advances. Such helps secured through the advance in values can be realized only in the vicinity of dense population and large commercial interests. With the sum realized the present magnificent farm of two hundred and fifty-four acres has been purchased, farm house and barn erected, equipment and every facility for research work provided, and all without the appropriation of a single dollar by the state.

The Geological and Natural History Survey.

An important adjunct of the scientific work of the University is the Geological and Natural History Survey of the State. This was organized in 1872 and placed under the direction of the Board of Regents. It still continues—a quarter of a century of scientific research conducted by a state upon its own domain. The original cost of this work was $1,000 per year; this was soon increased to $2,000, and in 1875, and subsequently, a quantity of Salt Spring lands, 38,643 acres, was turned over to the Regents to be disbursed in accordance with the law ordering the survey. This land at the minimum price of $5.00 per acre, for which it could be sold, will eventually enable the Regents to realize over $200,000. The amount already sold has brought over $75,000. The cash appropriations which the state has at various times voted for the maintenance of this work amount at date to $50,000, not including cost of printing.

The General Museum—A Zoological Alcove.

The survey is comprehensive in its scope. The fields of investigation named in the original act are geology, botany, zoology and meteorology. Two maps, a geologic and topographic, were also provided for; the latter, on approval, to become the official map of the state. A museum was also contemplated, which should exhibit to the people of the commonwealth in an orderly and scientific way its natural resources as discovered by the survey.

The geological exploration of the state was first prosecuted. Botany, zoology, meteorology and topography are to follow, in order, unless economy and efficiency can be secured by joint operations. The results of these investigations thus far available, are to be found in a series of annual reports covering almost a quarter of a century of geologic work; three volumes of the final report on the geology of the state; two brief reports of the State Zoologist, accompanied by a study of the birds of Minnesota by Dr. P. L. Hatch, and a synopsis of the Entomostraca of Minnesota by C. L. Herrick and C. H. Turner; one report of the State Botanist, containing an exhaustive review of the Metaspermæ of the Minnesota river valley; a series of bulletins, containing geological, botanical and zoological papers, besides many scientific papers from less comprehensive fields of study.

The steadiness of purpose which from the first has been a marked feature of the government of the University, has held the Geological and Natural History Survey to its work. After twenty-five years of uninterrupted research, a still longer period of useful investigation lies before the several departments of the University charged with the prosecution of this work thus far so successfully carried on.

Grants, Appropriations and Gifts.

The first condition of success in the development of any institution is the financial one. It is well at this point to note with what resources the University has been endowed. They have been derived from three sources.

First, Congressional appropriations; Second, Legislative appropriations; Third, Individual gifts and endowments.

Congressional Appropriations.

The Congress, in February, 1851, one day after the approval by Governor Ramsey of the legislative act creating the University of the Territory of Minnesota authorized the Secretary of the Interior to set apart two townships, 46,080 acres, for the use and support of the University of the Territory of Minnesota. In 1857 there was appropriated an additional two townships consisting of a like amount. In

The General Museum—The Herbarium.

1862 the historic Morrill bill made a grant to the State of Minnesota of 120,000 acres. In 1887, $15,000 annually was appropriated for the establishment and maintenance of an Agricultural Experiment Station. In 1890, $15,000 annually was appropriated, also for agriculture, with an additional $1,000 each year until the total should reach $25,000, at which figure the appropriation shall stand until otherwise ordered by Congress.

Of the above, much of the earlier grants was swept away in the financial disasters preceding and attending the civil war. The few hundred acres saved from these and the lands accruing under the Morrill bill have substantially all been sold and the sum invested in interest-bearing securities. This interest, with the $36,000 a year under the appropriation acts of 1887 and 1889, represents the income from government grants and appropriations.

State Appropriations. It can be said to the glory of the commonwealth that whenever called upon by the Regents, aid has been voted without complaint and with practical unanimity, to the full extent of the request or to the last dollar the state could properly command in support of the institution. Some of the more important special appropriations may be summarized:

Between 1867 and 1881 for construction:

1867.	Repairing the University building...	$15,000
1870.	Further repairs on the building...	10,000
1873.	Appropriation for erecting a front part to the same, and a building for College of Agriculture...	50,000
1881.	A six years' appropriation, of $30,000 per year..................................	180,000

$255,000

Owing to calamities which befell the state, the last appropriation was not drawn upon until 1883 and following years.

Between 1891 and 1895 for construction:

1891.	Appropriation for	Departments of Law and Medicine........................	$ 80,000
1893.	"	" Library and Assembly Hall.......................	175,000
1893.	"	" Workshops at the Farm.............................	30,000
1895.	"	" Dining Hall at the Farm...........................	42,000
1895.	"	" Dairy Hall.	15,000
1895.	"	" Blacksmith Shop......................................	7,000
1895.	"	" Laboratory of the Medical Sciences.............	40,000
1895.	"	" Astronomical Observatory..........................	10,000
1895.	"	" The Armory...	75,000

Total, $474,000

It will be noted that there was appropriated for new buildings between 1891 and 1895 more than twice as much as during all the preceding years. If 1884, the year in which the change in administration occurred, be taken as the divide, only $114,000 had been actually expended, while since that date $620,000 represents the state's investment in buildings alone, or more than five times the earlier amount.

For the libraries:

1891.	Appropriation for the several libraries..		$10,000
1895.	"	" General Library....................................	20,000

Total, $30,000

Some special appropriations:

1891.	Appropriation for establishing the School of Mining and Metallurgy.......		$6,000
1891.	"	" opening a Department of Pharmacy................	5,000
1891.	"	" salaries, Electrical Engineering and Mining, annually..	4,500
1895.	"	" maintenance, School Mining and Metallurgy, " ..	5,000

Some points to be noted in the appropriation by the State from year to year are as follows: In 1878 an annual tax of one-tenth of a mill was voted with an assessed valuation that year of nearly $230,000,000. But in

1881 the income was insufficient, and there was added............................ $	23,000
1885 The sum appropriated was increased per year to...........................	35,000
1887 the sum appropriated for annual support was changed to....................	50,000
1889 there was voted for additional allowance..................................	25,000
1893 a tax of 3-20 mill was voted; assessed valuation for that year about 635,000,000	
1895 an urgent deficiency bill added..	60,000

The significance of the foregoing lies in the fact that the University has grown at such a rapid and uninterrupted rate that even "the oldest" legislator has not

—13—

The Armory

been able since 1880 to appropriate enough for its needs, even by voting at three different times a special additional amount. At the present time a deficiency is throwing its shadow across the path of the Regents. The total of all current expenses from 1867 to the close of the year 1895-6, a period of thirty years, will not be far from $2,700,000. The total yearly enrollment for the same time will reach 19,139. The average cost per student, per annum, to the State is, therefore, $141.12. If the year 1884 again be taken as a dividing line between two groups of figures, we shall have:

Current expenses of the University, 1867-1884	$ 656,839.65
Total yearly enrollment, 1867-1884	5,163
Average annual cost per student	126.44
Current expenses, 1885-1896	2,043,777.89
Total yearly enrollment, 1885-1896	13,976
Average annual cost per student	146.27

The Students' Christian Association Building.

It may properly be mentioned that over forty-two per cent of the total enrollment up to 1884 consisted of preparatory students. Absolute accuracy in the above calculations is impossible, because some of the early current expenses were mingled with building and repair accounts, and some of the Geological and Natural History Survey expenses cannot be separated from University items. Again, many students are here for only a portion, great or small, of the University year.

In 1851, when the University was first thought of as a possible power in the development of the future commonwealth, the size and cost of such an institution were not dreamed of. State universities were scarcely known at that time, and none of them were expensive. Michigan was only a few years old and thus seemed chiefly a promise. *Quantum tempora mutaverunt!* The University was originally

established on "the proceeds of all land that may hereafter be granted by the United States."

Individual Gifts to the University. The first gift of this character was that of Franklin Steele, already noted. In 1857 and thereabouts there were made many loans, subscriptions and gifts by individual members of the Board of Regents and citizens resident in Minneapolis. These reached a total of a few thousand dollars. In 1872 there was donated by the friends of the University the sum of $720 towards securing for the museum a series of Ward's casts of fossils. From the establishment of the general library to the present time many books, pamphlets and manuscripts have been presented and bequeathed to this department of the University work. The total number of accessions of this character now amounts to hundreds of titles.

The alumni of the University in 1887 created an Alumni Fellowship which has been maintained up to the present time by personal subscriptions. This fund pays $250 per year, and through its expenditure a succession of Fellows in various

Y. M. C. A. Reading Room.

scientific and literary lines has been ensured. In 1893 the Albert Howard Scholarship was bequeathed which yields about $160 a year for such recipient as the Executive Committee shall designate on recommendation of the general Faculty. In 1892 the friends of the late Professor Moses Marston endowed a scholarship in English which is annually awarded to deserving scholarly attainment in English language and literature. The class of 1889 contributed funds, the income of which should be devoted to the payment of an annual memorial prize in history. In 1895 a College Fellowship was announced in the College of Engineering, Metallurgy and the Mechanic Arts to yield $200 annually. In 1891 the Gillette-Herzog Manufacturing Company, of Minneapolis, offered for competition by the students of the College of Engineering, Metallurgy and the Mechanic Arts two prizes: The first, $50 and a gold medal; and the second, $30 and a gold medal. Theses in competition are admitted from mechanical, structural, municipal and electrical engineering lines. The prizes have been most earnestly competed for by the students of the successive classes. They are of great importance in encouraging engineers to the most careful and scientific work in preparation of original designs.

Ore-Testing and Milling Laboratories.

We now pass to another class of gifts. In 1885 and following years the Christian friends of the University throughout the state subscribed for the erection of a building for the Students' Christian Association the sum of $12,000, which structure should be consecrated as the head-quarters of all Christian work and enterprise radiating from the institution. The movement leading to this was begun some time before the active canvass of 1885 and 1886 when the sum necessary for the construction was reached. The building was dedicated, free of debt, in 1887. Among the largest givers stand the names of Thomas Lowry, with $2,500; Fred Marquand, $2,000; Richard Chute, $1,000; John S. Pillsbury, $1,000; H. G. Harrison, $500; Chas. A. Pillsbury, $500; Cyrus Northrop, $500. About $1,450 was raised in St. Paul, but the names of the donors are not at hand.

The Furnace Room.

In 1892, through a committee consisting of E. M. Johnson, P. D. McMillan, Geo. H. Warren, Jas. R. Thorpe and S. C. Gale, the citizens of Minneapolis gener-

Pillsbury Hall.

ously subscribed over $5,000 for the erection of the Ore-Testing and Milling laboratories of the School of Mining and ·Metallurgy. Architect Harry W.

Pillsbury Hall—The Aquaria.

Jones gave the plans for the building, which now affords facilities for students in mining superior to those of any other institution in the United States. The equipment of these laboratories is superb. The entire plant cost about $17,000.

In 1884 Ex-Governor John S. Pillsbury endowed the institution with his munificent gift, Pillsbury Hall, equipped and furnished for work in natural history. This is by far the noblest gift to education within the history of the state. It is doubly prized by the community because it came at a time when the University was in sore need and when the state, in distress for want of funds, could not meet a need so plainly seen. At this time there were a few misguided citizens who urged the separation of the Agricultural College from the other departments of the University. Since it was through Regent Pillsbury's efforts that this union had been brought about and maintained for so many years, it was but natural that he should in tendering the gift express his heart's desire that the union might be lasting and ask that Pillsbury Hall might become the seal of a mutual pledge. In recognition the legislature passed a fitting preamble and resolutions, and through a large legislative committee placed them in the donor's hands. They follow:

WHEREAS, We recognize with gratitude the long and valued services rendered to our State University by

HONORABLE JOHN S. PILLSBURY

WHEREAS, Information has been conveyed to this Legislature by him of his purpose to donate to

THE UNIVERSITY OF MINNESOTA

a sum of money aggregating one hundred and fifty thousand dollars; therefore,

Resolved, By the House of Representatives, the Senate concurring, that for this large and munificent donation we tender to Mr Pillsbury this expression of our sincere gratitude.

Resolved, That we accept this splendid gift with the solemn assurance of this Legislature that the unity of the several departments of the University shall always be preserved, and that the Agricultural College shall be maintained as an important department.

Resolved, That we hereby convey the individual pledges of the members of this Legislature that the interests of the University shall be carefully guarded in the future.

The foregoing was signed by the President of the Senate, Speaker of the House of Representatives and the individual members of the Senate and House committees.

Another gift, that of Honorable Frederick Weyerhauser, is the guarantee of the salary of the Professor of Semitic Languages and History for the period of five years, beginning with the year 1895-96.

Thus it is seen that for an institution which has not graduated its twenty-fourth class, the University of Minnesota indeed has many loyal and warm-hearted, generous friends.

INTERNAL AFFAIRS.

We shall now discuss those incidents in the internal life of the University which have had a moulding effect in its development as an institution of learning and as the central educational plant in the intellectual development of Minnesota. It has been truly said that the difference between a college and university is always one of aim. The college devotes itself to the academic schooling of young men and women; the university must exert itself in every field of intellectual activity which its environment projects. This consideration has controlled the growth of the University to a larger degree than has been the case in any other institution of learning in America. That was the real issue in the memorable contest over the "Plan of Organization" in the early 70's, although it is doubtful whether the men who fought against the plan realized it. The University idea predominated. And it is the University idea peculiar to America; not that of England with its emphasis on culture and classical breadth, nor of Germany with its erudition, but the real American idea of capability; that is, that he who educates himself to do the most, whatever be his line of activity, educates himself into the best condition of American citizenship.

The act of 1860 providing for the government and regulation of the University directed that there should be attached a Collegiate Department in which regular college classes should be formed. The reorganization act of February 18, 1868, now regarded as the Charter of the University, further provided for the establishment of five or more colleges or departments: First, a department of Elementary Instruction; second, a College of Science, Literature and the Arts; third, a College of Agriculture and the Mechanic Arts, including Military Tactics; fourth, a College or Department of Law, and fifth, a College or Department of Medicine.

The University Book Store.

The department of Elementary Instruction had already been in successful operation since October 7, preceding under the designation of Preparatory Department. Upon the arrival of Col. Folwell in 1869, a careful study of the situation was made by him, eminent educators were consulted and a proposition marked out and laid before the Regents. This was called the "Plan of Organization." From first to last it has been subjected to much criticism. Many warmly approved it as adapted to the needs of the time; others were adverse to it as a fundamental measure. As the events centering about that "plan" are brought in review it appears that the chief objection was not the lack of merit in the plan itself, but in the educational prejudices of those who had to work under its requirements and tendencies. Its essential features were these: The Department of Elementary Instruction should consist of five years, one year designated the

Latin School, soon to be discontinued, and four years as the Collegiate Department, the third and fourth of which corresponded very nearly with the freshman and sophomore years of the older American colleges; the work comprised under junior and senior years should constitute the College of Science, Literature and the Arts; the professional and technical courses — Law, Medicine, Civil Engineering, Mechanical Engineering and Agriculture were to be of equal rank in the preparation required, time devoted and in every other possible respect. This feature made the College of Science, Literature and the Arts the department of learning and scholarly acquirements. It thus became, in a sense, a professional school, to be developed as the future demands and resources of the State should direct. It was spoken of as "The University Course in Arts" and all students were strongly urged to continue through one of its courses of study before entering upon further professional preparation.

Sanitary Science—Laboratory.

It was a part of the plan that the studies of both the Latin School and the Collegiate Department should be dropped off as fast as the high schools could take the work. In the minds of the supporters of the plan the foregoing points were decidedly advantageous in view of the condition of education in a state only twelve years old, and with a population of less than 440,000; while in the opinion of others, advantage would lie in placing the well-tried New England plan of an American college upon the new commonwealth. Whether the "Plan" attained the specific ends aimed at by

The Ladies' Parlor.

its eminent promoter or not, ideas and principles intimately associated with it have become so impressed upon the state that Minnesota today boasts of the best educational system in the United States.

The steps of progress in the growth of the University during President Folwell's administration, 1869-1884, are the following:

I. The adoption of the Plan of Organization under which was developed the University rather than the College.

II. The rise, culmination and partial excision of the Preparatory Department.

III. The close relationship perfected between the University and the high schools of the state through the creation, March 3, 1881, of the State High School Board "constituted

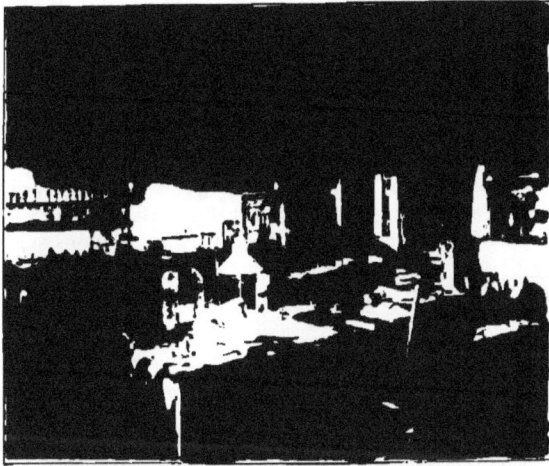

Chemistry—Dr. Frankforter's Private Laboratory.

Department of Physics—A Laboratory.

a Board of Commissioners on Preparatory Schools for the encouragement of higher education in this state."

It must be borne in mind that educational progress never moves forward in a direct line; many notions once regarded as fundamental disappear; new ideas become engrafted on the system. The up-building under the best of circumstances is a slow process. Misgivings and obstacles everywhere intervene. Yet in the history of this institution, thanks to the three or four strong and unflinching personalities directing its affairs, the advance has been steady and almost uninterrupted since the reorganization act came into full force and effect.

The discussion of the plan of organization continued. To some extent it fell into the narrow field of mutual recrimination. The Regents in their endeavor to adjust difficulties, asked for opinions. None of sufficient weight were presented against what had become the policy of the institution; therefore a resolution was passed by the Board suggesting some minor revisions but distinctly stating that "the Board are ot the opinion, after carefully considering the many questions, sug-

Chemical and Physical Laboratories.

gestions and recommendations made, that it is inexpedient to interfere with the essential features of the plan."

But those minor revisions were the rub. The more the Faculty tried to revise the more perplexing became the situation. The catalogues of a series of years following 1872 show a succession of changes made apparently, not on the merit or the thing changed, but on the massing of votes in the Faculty. Latin, Greek, mathematics and philosophy were firmly entrenched, because the work was thoroughly disciplinary and in the hands of able teachers. These departments were never weakened in any readjustment. Teachers trained for other work had not then graduated. Recognizing that any course of study is what its teachers make it, we understand why so-called scientific and modern language courses were weak. There were no scientists to be had in those days. German and French were merely means to an end, and that end was not intellectual culture. The Professor of Philosophy wrote and taught a text-book in German; geology, mineralogy, physical geography, botany, zoology, physiology, entomology, etc., etc., were all in charge of the "Professor of Chemistry and Instructor in Natural Sciences and in French."

As time went on matters did not improve. It was a critical period. The plan had been adopted; the Regents were very patient. Nothing of greater value or of greater sceming advantage to all interests in the state had been proposed. The suggestion of a committee that something like the American college course be substituted, was met by the following resolution, penned by the soldier hand of Gen.

Physics—Apparatus Room.

Sibley: "It is the judgment of this Board that it is not expedient to make any radical change or modification in the settled policy of the University as heretofore fixed by the Board," and unanimously adopted. The Regents became more

Physics—A Lecture Room.

and more convinced that drastic measures must be adopted. Harmony in counsel was essential to successful development of the internal—the real—strength of the institution. At last, and to every appearance without any preconcerted signal or concert of action, the Regents convened in annual meeting in May, 1880. The balloting for the Faculty began. When, on the evening of the second day of the session, adjournment was taken, seven out of a faculty of eleven members of high rank were not returned. A committee had been appointed to secure and report names for the vacancies. This work was done in a most thorough and satisfactory manner.

Following the momentous event of 1880 were four years of remarkable peace and prosperity. Every department was engaged in quiet and effective work. The number of students increased twenty-eight per cent; the number of instructors doubled, from fifteen to thirty; the courses of study were extended and strengthened. All traces of the storm disappeared and the work of internal development

Chemistry—A Laboratory.

went on. Concord and mutual helpfulness pervaded all councils. President Folwell then resolved to lay down executive work and devote himself to a cherished line of teaching and research. He accordingly resigned March 8th, 1883. His resignation was accepted, the same to take effect when his successor should be elected and qualified. The Regents, realizing the delicacy and weight of their responsibility, began their search for a man to fill the place. They made no mistake. The right man was found and secured. Cyrus Northrop, Professor of English Literature in Yale College, was invited to visit Minneapolis and the University. It was the glad old story; seeing was believing. President Northrop entered upon his duties September 2d, 1884, and was formally inaugurated June 11th, 1885.

Below are the figures showing the material University at the time of the graduation of the first class; the institution which Dr. Folwell passed to his successor, and its condition at the last commencement, periods eleven years apart:

	1873	1884	1895
Number of graduate students enrolled..	0	10	88
Number of undergraduates in regular classes	72	97	1,986
Number of preparatory in regular classes.....	204	59	0
Number of specials in regular classes............	16	121	185
Number of professors.............	7	16	91
Number of instructors.................................	3	7	35
Number of lecturers........................ .. ..,......	0	1	16
Number of University scholars......................	0	0	23
Number of fellows...................................	0	0	3
Number of colleges of the University...........	2	4	7
The salary account.................................. $	19,907.50	$ 31,130.84	$ 169,880.77
Total current expense account..........	24,577.80	64,604.93	254,117.98
Estimated value of the " Plant"............	55,000.00	250,000.00	1,800,000.00
Capital represented at 3 per cent. the interest at which bonds are now placed	875,000.00	2,400,000.00	10,275,000.00

These figures speak. They show a most remarkable growth. Every Minnesotan is proud of it.

Psychology—The Lecture Room.

The Collegiate Department.

The above name given to the Department of Elementary Instruction provided for in the organic law of the institution, by virtue of a by-law of the Board of Regents, was in early years the most conspicuous feature of the University. It was actually instituted October 7th, 1867, when preparatory work was for the third time opened. It consisted of two divisions: First, the Latin School.

This was an organization of elementary work for the purpose of preparing for the fourth class of the collegiate courses of study; it was discontinued in 1873. The Second, the Collegiate Department proper. The standard of admission to this department was elementary algebra, Latin grammar and reader. It aimed to include the work of an ordinary college through the sophomore year. It emphasized the tendency apparent twenty-five years ago, to make the junior year the starting point for professional training. While many things were said as to future intentions regarding the Collegiate Department, emphasis lay on the proposition to drop the work year by year just as fast as the high schools could take it up. The University would then consist of junior and senior years, together with the work built upon them.

That the Collegiate Department played an important part in the growth of the University is apparent from the enrollment records. It was not

Department of Zoology—The General Laboratory.

until 1880 that the first and second classes, sophomore and freshman, exceeded in numbers the third and fourth, and up to that year the enrollment of the Collegiate Department constituted eighty-three per cent of the entire attendance. From that time until 1890 preparatory work rapidly declined, and in the last named year the last preparatory student was advanced into the freshman class.

Meanwhile it had become apparent that the original numbering of the classes could n)t well be maintained. They were called first, second, etc., for a number of years. In 1879 the terms sub-freshman, freshman and sophomore became synonyms of the words third, second and first, by which, previously, the several classes had been designated. In that same year the fourth class was discontinued. By 1890 the high schools of the state had become so thoroughly organized under the wise foresight and administration of the State High School Board that full preparation for the University could be carried by them.

Meanwhile the organization which had been so useful was, in a measure, outgrown. It was clearly recognized by Faculty and Regents that many years must elapse before freshman and sophomore years could be handed over to the high schools, and University work could be begun at the commencement of the junior year. The natural result of such a condition was the gradual disappearance of the distinction between collegiate and university as defining terms and the merging of the work of both organizations into

The College of Science, Literature and the Arts.

The internal history of the College of Science, Literature and the Arts is a record of rapid progress and advancement to a foremost place among American universities. The broad policy recognized at the outset has been kept in view; the traditions of the institution, which are traditions of progress, have been steadily adhered to. Bright and able men have represented the several departments of instruction; they have carried their work steadily forward, their opinions

Plant Morphology—A Laboratory.

have been liberal, their ideas progressive, and the whole management of the college has been distinguished by elasticity and strength. The original plan was to recognize the equality of the courses in science and literature with the established classical course of American colleges.

The Elective System. The elective system was incorporated with the first course of study proposed for the College of Science, Literature and the Arts; so there has never been such an event as the *introduction* of electives any more than there has been the admission of women. Marked advances have been made from time to time in the application of such work. The several stages in this advance may thus be summarily stated:

In 1871, when the Regents issued their first schedule of studies for graduation, thirty-three per cent of the work in the College of Science, Literature and the Arts was elective in all three courses offered, viz., arts, science, and literature. Nearly

The Observatory.

The Telescope.

equal freedom was permitted in the scientific and literary courses of the Collegiate Department. In 1874 the system was still further extended by multiplying subjects from which the electives could be selected, until the third term of senior year, when only one subject was required; thus, thirty-nine per cent of the work was optional. In 1880 a still further expansion was voted, by introducing a larger number of elective studies and reducing the prescribed work to one subject only. In 1879 there were also certain modifications, in that the students in all three courses were required to pursue the same subject. This move of the Faculty was to emphasize their intention to maintain complete equality between the several courses so far as disciplinary value could be secured in the instruction offered. In 1885 the senior year was made wholly elective, inasmuch as at that time the number of subjects was changed from three, each of five hours per week, to four, each of four hours per week, the required work fell to 12½ per cent of the whole amount. In 1892 the last step was taken, by declaring all work of the junior and senior years elective—the only bar excluding any student from any department being the lack of preparation to perform satisfactory work.

In 1888 another change was made of far-reaching importance. The existing plan of long courses in the sciences for the scientific course, with a free choice between physics and chemistry in physical lines, and between botany and zoology in biological lines, was established. From that time the scientific course has been as distinctly disciplinary as have the classical and literary courses. The ground for this step lay in the belief that, first of all, it is discipline and not information that should be secured through the student's efforts. The change, instead of being revolutionary, was simply in the direction of universal opinion, and a recognition that preparation for life's duties lay in the field of natural phenomena as well as of human customs and accomplishment. Wisdom is justified of her children.

The Observatory.

In the 70's an effort to develop astronomy almost succeeded. A strong movement was made to secure a small working observatory on precisely the plan now carried out.

1891 saw the erection of a small transit-house, equipped with transit-circle, astronomical clock, chronograph, etc., and 1895 was the date of the completion of the Students' Observatory, made possible by legislative action. Its equipment consists of a ten inch equatorial of one hundred and fifty inches focal length. This instrument has three objectives, one combination of which forms the visual telescopic objective, and another the photographic objective. There are also three eyepieces of different magnifying powers, a filar micrometer and a driving clock. Two reading microscopes are provided for reading the declination circles, and the guiding telescope is of four inch aperture. A spectroscope and photograph measuring machine are among the instruments.

The Library.

This is the pride of the University; it also marks an epoch in the progress of literary work. The building contains the administrative offices, the Assembly Hall, seating eight hundred people, the library with its large reading room, together with four departments of instruction, English language and literature, economics and politics, history and philosophy. Each department has its suite of studies for instructors, seminars for advanced work, and class rooms. The interior is char-

Library—The Chapel.

Library—The President's Office.

acterized by admirable convenience for work. It is of fire proof construction throughout. Its exterior is purely classic. The dimensions are, 194 feet long, 135 feet wide and two stories bigb. The building without and within is the most beautiful thus far constructed. Among the special features may be mentioned the entrance with its broad stairway leading to the cortile from which students proceed to the departments of economics and English and to the large general reading room of the Library. This reading room is 44 feet in width, 100 feet in depth and 33 feet high, and accommodates one hundred and fifty readers. An enriched entablature extends around both cortile and reading room.

The Armory.

In 1883 there was erected upon the west end of the campus a drill hall, called by common consent the Coliseum. It contained one of the largest audience rooms in the West. In 1894 this building burned to the ground. The legislature of 1895 voted $75,000 to replace the Coliseum by an Armory, which should serve its purpose as a drill hall for the cadet battalion and an assembly hall for the large gatherings of special University occasions. In September, 1895, the Regents adopted the plans of Architect Charles R. Aldrich, and work was immediately begun. The building will contain an audience room for 4,000 persons. It will be three stories high. A sufficient number of rooms will thus be secured for the classes in military science and physical culture including the necessary offices.

The exterior is very plain, carrying just enough of ornamentation to make it pleasing to the eye. The front is broken by a large massive tower, Norman in style, giving to it a decidedly military aspect.

Some Departments of Instruction.

It may be well at this point to note a few of the departments which have developed in the College of Science, Literature and the Arts within the last dozen years. In brief review we note that the department of mathematics, which was first under the charge of Professor Ira Moore, became for a brief time the care of Arthur Beardsley, but was directed from 1870 until 1880 by Professor Edwin J. Thompson. It included astronomy. In 1880 Professor Downey was called; in 1893 Arthur Edwin Haynes came as assistant professor. Francis P. Leavenworth came in 1892 to devote himself especially to astronomy. He is now director of the Observatory.

Latin and Greek have maintained a steady growth. W. W. Wasbburn, principal in 1867-69 was the first professor of Greek. On his resignation Jabez Brooks was elected August 23, 1869. John C. Hutchinson is associate professor.

The first professor of Latin was Versal J. Walker, who died May 18, 1876. In 1878 R. H. Tripp took the chair for two years. John S. Clark has taught Latin since 1876, becoming professor of the Latin language and literature in 1886.

During the current year a chair of Semitic languages and history has been established. Professor James Richard Jewett was called to the work. Hebrew, Arabic and Oriental languages and history are being taught.

Philosophy flourished under Gabriel Campbell until 1880. Alexander T. Ormond followed him for three years, after whom Thomas Peebles, John Dewey and Williston S. Hough came in order before Frederick J. E. Woodbridge. Psychology has received attention for three years at the hands of James R. Angell and Harlow S. Gale.

Armory—Floor Plans.

The modern languages have prospered. Professor Campbell first taught German; July 29, 1874 John G. Moore was elected assistant professor of the German language and literature; in the following year he was professor of North European languages. He is now professor of the German language and literature. French in early years was united with history and subsequently with German. In 1880 Charles W. Benton began to teach. At the meeting of the Regents held June 26, 1872, a petition was received from many influential Scandinavians for the establishment of a Scandinavian department. This paper was filed because the resources of the University would not permit the step. On March 2, 1883, the professorship of Scandinavian language and literature was created by legislative enactment. Only Olaus J. Breda has filled it.

The English language was first taught by Aris B. Donaldson, whose chair was rhetoric and English literature. In 1874 Moses Marston succeeded him, performing excellent work until his lamented death, which occurred July 11, 1883. In the spring of 1884 George E. MacLean succeeded to the chair. He occupied it until

Chemistry—A Lecture Room.

1895. The existing features of the work, both in the English language and in literature are in large measure due to his erudition and constant enthusiasm. Rhetoric and elocution, under the charge of Maria L. Sanford since 1880, assisted by E. E. McDermott since 1890, constitute two groups of the present federated courses in English.

The department of history shows equally well with that of economics, the steady advance of the College of Science, Literature and the Arts. There were probably not more than one or two chairs of history in American colleges when this college received its first junior class September 5, 1871. In 1874 Richard W. Laing was appointed assistant professor in charge of history and elocution. With his retirement in 1879 the work went to Professors Campbell and Moore for one year. Professor Ormond received the work in 1880, and his successor in philoso-

Botany—A Laboratory.

Chemistry—Gas Analysis Laboratory.

phy, Thomas Peebles, taught it for two years from 1883. Harry P. Judson was elected professor of history and lecturer on pedagogy in 1885. For seven years the department of history grew rapidly. Willis M. West came as assistant professor in 1893. In 1895 he was promoted to the chair he now fills.

Economics and politics, taught from the early days of the institution by President Folwell, assumed greater importance when as professor of political science he began to devote his whole time to the work in 1885. It is now a prominent department of University work. Since 1892 the work has extended through the junior and senior years.

A line of work encouraging both in present condition and promise is the teachers' course. A lectureship in pedagogy was established at the coming of Professor Judson in 1885. In 1891 State Superintendent David L. Kiehle became lecturer. In two years the demand for more extended work in pedagogy became so pronounced that the chair of pedagogy was created, and Dr. Kiehle as professor entered upon the work of building up a permanent teachers' course. This is of two years' length. The studies laid out are such as can be pursued in the regular University classes. The enrollment has been as follows: For 1893, 22 teachers; 1894, 29; 1895, 46, and 1896, 46.

The military department brings into its work every ablebodied student and many of uncertain

Chemistry—The Library and Balance Room.

strength. Lieutenant Harry A. Leonhauser has been preceded by a long line of brave soldiers and capable teachers.

Among the sciences, so-called, chemistry is the oldest in that it took on definite shape as a department of study and research first among them all. In 1869 it was located in the old University building where room twenty-seven and the stairway now are. It was in charge of Professor Twining who had to teach many other things. This gentlemen is said to have been one of the most accomplished men the University ever held. Soon Professor Strange took the chair. He too moved on. Professor Thompson succeeded him for a day. We read: "Resolved that Prof. E. J. Thompson be declared to be the professor of mathematics and therefore is hereby relieved from the chair of chemistry to which he was yesterday assigned." The work was placed in the hands of the most persistant defender of the scientific cult which the University ever had. That chemistry is strong in the institution today in every way is largely due to the ability and scientific zeal of Stephen F. Peckham, who filled this chair between 1873 and 1880.

In 1875 the department moved into the Agricultural College building, which stood until its destruction by fire, where the building devoted to chemistry and physics now stands. James A. Dodge was professor of chemistry between 1880 and 1893. In October of the last named year George B. Frankforter was called to the department and a rapid growth has followed.

Physics was first in charge of Professor Peckham. From 1875 to 1880 Louis W. Peck held the position of assistant professor of physics. From 1880 to 1885 William A. Pike was in charge. In the last named year Frederick S. Jones took the work as instructor. In 1889 the chair was assigned him which he at present occupies. The work of the Department of Physics was, in the first years of electrical engineering, closely associated with that course.

Lithological Laboratory.

Geology and mineralogy were under the charge of the State Geologist from 1872 until 1878, when that officer asked to be relieved from teaching duties that he might devote his entire time to the prosecution of the geological survey. This request being granted, Christopher W. Hall was secured to take the classroom duties, and serve in the field as assistant geologist. He came in April, 1878, and in 1879 was made Professor of Geology, Mineralogy and Biology.

Department of Zoology—A Laboratory.

Biology has been turned over to more modern hands. The beginning of existing laboratory methods, as applied along biological lines, must date from

1873. In that year the Executive Committee was "instructed to purchase a microscope for the use of the University, not to exceed in cost $100." That same instrument, after twenty-three years of constant use and much inflicted with repairs, is still in the service of the geological survey.

In 1884 Clarence S. Herrick was instructor in biology; 1885 saw Henry F. Nachtrieb in that capacity, but devoting particular attention to zoology. In 1886 he was assistant professor of biology, and in 1888 professor of animal biology. In the same year he was appointed state zoologist on the geological and natural history survey.

In 1887 Conway MacMillan came as instructor in botany; 1890 saw him

The Library—General Reading Room.

advanced to an assistant professorship and the position of state botanist. In 1892 he occupied the chair of botany.

With the gift of Pillsbury Hall; the erection of the building devoted to chemistry and physics; the arrangement of the four scientific subjects, botany, chemistry, physics and zoology, in four parallel long courses; the securing of good, progressive teachers and the adoption of a liberal policy on the part of the administration of the University has exerted a remarkable influence upon the institution as a whole. That influence is not of "science" taught, but the scientific method applied. Every department feels the effects. Therein lies the secret of the rapid advancement of all lines of scholarly work.

Chemistry—Dr. Frankforter's Office.

The Library—Registrar's Office.

The Graduate Department.

From the very adoption of the plan, the transferring to the high schools of the lower branches of university work has been the settled policy. The institution has also been preparing to give instruction, and indeed, is now giving it to graduates who desire to carry their studies further than the limits of an ordinary curriculum allow. This work, so long as the resources of the institution are as small as at present in proportion to the number of students thronging its classrooms, must necessarily be subordinated to pressing duties. Still a goodly number of departments have made most commendable progress in attracting graduates to the University. Not only in the College of Science, Literature and the Arts, but in the College of Engineering, Metallurgy and the Mechanic Arts and in the College of Law many are enrolled.

Library—The Cortile.

In engineering, attention is being given particularly to structural engineering, locomotive engineering, certain phases of electrical engineering and mining. But it is to the College of Science, Literature and the Arts that graduate students come in large numbers. The following table shows the attendance and choice of subjects during the current year in that college: English, 24; Romance and French, 14; German,

Botany—The Library.

12; Latin, 16; Greek, 7; Economics, 20; History, 32; Geology and Mineralogy, 12; Chemistry, 15; Physics, 11; Botany, 8; Zoology, 8; Psychology and Philosophy, 19; Scandinavian, 7; Astronomy, 3; Mathematics, 3; Pedagogy, 1; Semitic, 3; Military, 1.

—41—

Dean Hall's Office.

Chemistry—Sugar Laboratory.

College of Engineering, Metallurgy and the Mechanic Arts.

This College dates from the adoption of the plan of the University, July 12th, 1870. The organization was at that time the College of Agriculture and the Mechanic Arts and it was one of the two colleges first created. Arthur Beardsley, C. E., was the first professor. He held the chair of "Civil Engineering and Industrial Mechanics." In 1872 two courses of study were presented. civil engineering and mechanical engineering, each of two years' length. The professional subjects embraced in these courses were somewhat crude and meagre, inasmuch as we find mathematics, mechanics, modern languages, English literature, ethics, political economy, the fine arts, linguistics, drawing, shop work and surveying, all embodied in a two years' course of study. In 1873 Mitchell D. Rhame became

The Engineering Building.

instructor in civil engineering and physics and in the year following, professor of mechanical and civil engineering. In 1874 the College of Mechanic Arts was separated from the College of Agriculture. Until that year, 1874, the full degrees, Civil Engineer and Mechanical Engineer were offered. With the reorganization of the College of Mechanic Arts after the separation, the degree became that of bachelor in the respective engineering lines. In 1880, under a reorganization of some of the departments of the University, Professor Rhame retired, and William A. Pike was called to the chair of engineering, in charge of physics.

Professor Pike brought and put into operation a unique plan of shop work and elementary professional practice known as the Russian system—a system

The Carpenter Shop.

The Machine Shop.

planned solely for instruction, in which the knowledge obtained is that of principles and processes rather than towards proficiency in any particular trade. Space for this work was made in the basement of the Agricultural College building, which stood from 1874 to 1888 where now the building devoted to chemistry and physics stands. The testing laboratory was located in the basement of the old building,

The Engine Room.

where a fifty thousand pound Olsen machine was set up. The work soon outgrew its several quarters. Plans were proposed for a new building and soon took final shape In 1886 the present Engineering building was occupied and technical work became concentrated. With the occupancy of this building a marked impetus was given to engineering work. The Artisans' Training School was established and an additional line of usefulness was opened. This school, grouping several lines of special work, was a pioneer in the training of artisans. Though it has now been discontinued, during its existence it was especially helpful in directing the attention of the schools of the larger cities of the state to manual training courses. Wilbur F. Decker, Henry M. Waitt and W. Frank Carr proved very efficient assistants in this work. Mr. Decker assisted Professor Pike in the preparation of a Manual of Industrial Drawing still quite widely used. In 1885 William R. Hoag and John H. Barr were appointed instructors, the former of civil and the latter of mechanical engineering. These two men were successively promoted until in 1890 they were full professors in their respective departments. The following year brought the resignation of Professor Barr, and 1892 that of

Engineering—The Library.

Dean Pike, who opened an office in Minneapolis as a consulting engineer. For the twelve years during which Mr. Pike had been successively professor, director, and dean of the College of Mechanic Arts, he had rendered valuable service in the organization and upbuilding of the work. He remained one year with the College as lecturer. After his resignation there was united with the College of Mechanic

Civil Engineering—Apparatus Room.

Electrical Engineering—Dynamo Room.

Arts the School of Mining and Metallurgy and a course in technical chemistry was added. The organization, then called *The College of Engineering, Metallurgy and the Mechanic Arts*, consisted of courses in civil, mechanical and electrical engineering, architecture, mining, chemistry and metallurgy, with two courses in practical mechanics and a school of design, free-hand drawing and wood carving. In 1893 the course in architecture was discontinued, and in 1895, the school of design, free-hand drawing and wood carving was modified into a course in industrial art, in connection with the department of drawing to which Professor Kirchner came in the fall of 1894. This work has developed rapidly and the department now consists of four instructors giving courses in drawing, and twelve in elementary art and applied design. The School of Design built up through the personal efforts of Henry T. Ardley, its principal, occupied a field of great usefulness. But with the advance into technical lines of study and the heavy demands for funds in these directions a modification of the work of this school seemed necessary.

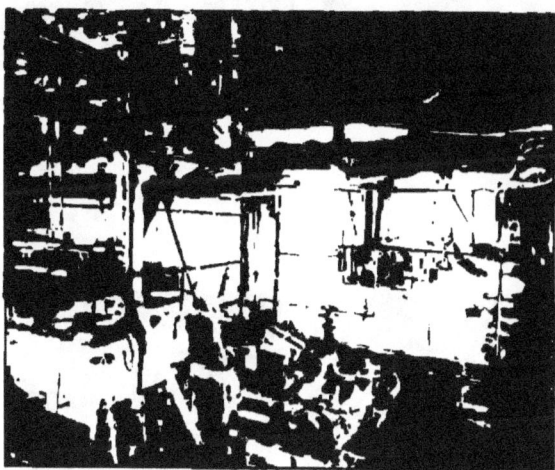

Amalgamation and Leaching Plants.

The several professional departments in this College are rapidly developing into lines of thorough professional training. The difference between the older courses in civil and mechanical engineering and those as they exist at present, in the proportion and scientific character of the professional work, is most marked. In the former, instruments of the highest precision are being secured and work of corresponding type is aimed at. The Topographical Survey of the state now attached to this department, is proving a laboratory of research work in civil engineering. Especial attention is also being given in this department to structural problems and designs. This work was expanded by Professor J. E. Wadsworth, from 1892 to 1895. Assistant Professor Frank II. Constant is now directing the work so ably developed by his predecessor.

In the mechanical field, what was high engineering a few years ago is now relegated to mechanics and mechanics' special courses, while testing and designing claim highest attention. True, the machine shop, pattern shop and engine room

Professor Appleby's Office.

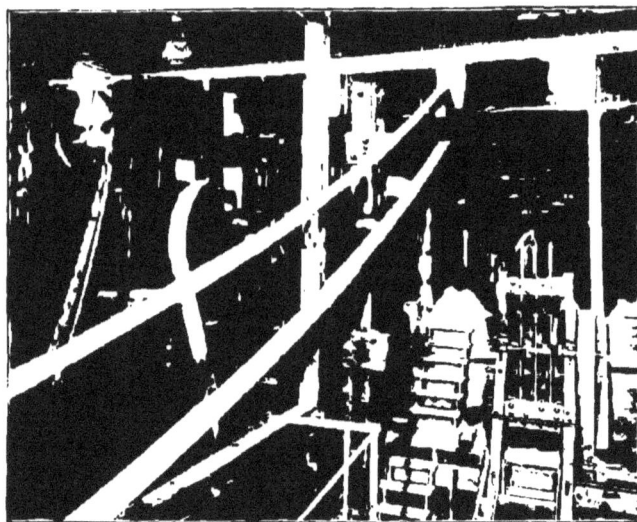

The Stamp Mills.

have been pushed forward in equipment and efficiency as rapidly as the resources of the University would permit. Yet it is a means to another and far higher end— the making of first-class engineers. Upon the resignation of Dean Pike, Instructor Harry E. Smith was made assistant professor and placed at the head of the department. In 1895 H. Wade Hibbard was called to the College as an assistant professor. While devoting attention to machine design he is developing important courses in locomotive engineering and car design.

Assay Laboratory.

Electrical engineering is new. The catalogue of 1887 makes first mention of this work as "a modification of the course in mechanical engineering." In two years substantial progress had been made, for we read, "Frederick S. Jones, A. B., instructor in electricity." In 1890 E. P Burch was assistant, and in the following year George D. Shepardson accepted the chair of electrical engineering. The remarkable advances of the last decade have marked out unexpected lines of usefulness in the field of electricity; already in 1891 this course had overtaken in number its older engineering associates. The annual enrollment has been, for 1889, 2; 1890, 6; 1891, 25; 1892, 45; 1893, 59; 1894, 64; 1895, 56; 1896, 78. It has proved an increasingly attractive field of engineering anticipation and enterprise. One of the interesting spots in this department is the dynamo room, containing engines, dynamos and motors to represent types in construction and adjustment, for special uses in the conservation and application of electrical power.

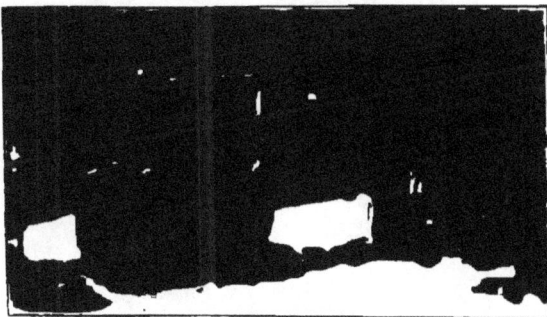

Coarse Concentration Plant.

Chemistry is one of the new fields for the training of technological skill. A course in chemical engineering was first offered in 1892. The science in its wide and paramount applications in the arts, brings constantly increasing demands upon those entering it as a profession. The engineer in this field must have a thorough preparation in mathematics, physics and metallurgy. Such preparation

Fine Crushing and Concentrating Plant.

Chlorination Plant.

he is here able to secure. It is interesting to note that this enterprise is opening a new field for the exercise of woman's skill and capability. Already several ladies have entered the course and are preparing themselves in a most enthusiastic way for this field of professional activity.

The School of Mining and Metallurgy was organized in 1889 to meet a demand for technical education of a kind called for in the development of the remarkable mining interests of the state. In 1891 William R. Appleby was elected professor of mining and metallurgy. The technical work of the school was thereupon opened. Its development has been such that in 1895 Frederick W. Denton, a mining engineer of much experience was called as associate of Professor Appleby. This call was also in response to the voice of the state as expressed in legislative action. In 1895, $5,000 per year additional for the maintenance of this school was almost unanimously appropriated. The assay laboratories and lecture rooms are located in Pillsbury Hall. The laboratories for ore testing are perhaps the especial features of this school. In these are modern

Crushing and Sampling Floor.

appliances on a commercial scale for testing ores of gold, silver and base metals. Stamping, concentration both coarse and fine, amalgamation, lixiviation and preparatory roasting are among the more prominent lines of examination and treatment to which ores are subjected.

With the arrival of Professor Denton another important line of professional preparation is made possible. Field work in mining and metallurgy is now conducted. Four weeks each of sophomore and junior years are given to mining work, mine surveying and the investigation of modern metallurgical plants. The annual enrollment of the school has been as follows: 1891, 3; 1892, 3; 1893, 17; 1894, 21; 1895, 24; and 1896, 36.

In 1894 the College was greatly strengthened by calling Henry T. Eddy to the chair of engineering and mechanics. An educator of wide experience, well-known as the author of many mathematical and physical papers, Dr. Eddy has already infused strength and enthusiasm to an encouraging degree.

The Dining Hall.

A function of this College which should here be recorded is the building up of technical libraries within the several professional departments. These are composed of the latest technical and general works, files of all the leading periodicals devoted to each particular subject, charts and other related material. A most excellent working library in a well arranged reading room, is to be found in the Engineering building. The libraries of chemistry, electrical engineering, geology, and mining and metallurgy are also sufficiently extensive to afford reference facilities for a wide range of research work.

The College of Agriculture.

The physical conditions of Minnesota have made agriculture an educational field of peculiar importance. It was named as one of the five departments constituting the University of the Territory of Minnesota in the act of 1851. In 1858

The Dining Hall.

"an Agricultural School by the name and style of the Agricultural College of the State of Minnesota" was organized, located two miles from where Glencoe now stands, and placed under the control of the State Agricultural Society. "The Agricultural College of Minnesota" resulted from an amendment to previous legislation approved March 2, 1865, and was designed to receive the lands donated to the state by Congress under the Morrill act. Three years later a further act was passed consolidating all grants for agriculture, placing the same in the hands of the Regents of the University of Minnesota, and repealing all earlier inconsistent legislation.

The College of Agriculture was one of the departments of the University thus re-created. A preparatory department of the college was opened in Septem-

ber, 1868, which enrolled fifteen students. The chair of practical and theoretical agriculture was established in 1869. The attendance in this department has never been large; indeed, no other result could be expected in an institution built as was this in a community living upon a soil so rich and varied, and
with land so cheap and return for labor so munificent that science was indeed a
luxury upon every farm in the commonwealth. One student took the course in
agriculture and graduated before President Northrop arrived. Many others had
entered, prosecuted their work for a time and then dropped out of the University
altogether or entered other colleges and prepared for professional life. The situation was one of solicitude in the deliberations of the Board of Regents for years.
They gave it their especial attention at the start. They had done everything that
could reasonably be done to make the work attractive and give the farmers' boys
the education they ought to receive in the way of preparation for farmers' work.
The door had been swung quite open and the way had been made plain. In 1874

The Library.

the President of the University advised that lectures in the College of Agriculture
"be open to all comers; that no conditions be put upon admission except a regis-
tration and a general pledge to punctual attendance." A plan in short which
"proposes to go to work without any theory; to take such students as can be
had and give them such instruction about their business as they desire to be given
and are competent to acquire." Such was the situation when President Northrop entered upon his work, and it continued practically unchanged until 1888.

The various lines of work in the College of Agriculture had at all times been in
the hands of competent men. Daniel A. Robertson was the first professor of agriculture. Upon his resignation the farm superintendent took charge. "Under his
judicious and industrious management the fencing of the farm [was] completed."
In 1872 Professor D. P. Strange was called. He was endowed with admirable
qualities. In 1874 he in turn was followed by Chas. Y. Lacy, and in 1880 Edward D.
Porter came to the College as professor of agriculture, to resign in 1888 and

accept the directorship of the Missouri Experiment Station. He was succeeded by Professor Willet M. Hayes who, although for two years away from the state, is the present incumbent. While the University course in agriculture includes considerable practical work, yet it is largely scientific. The four fundamental sciences in agriculture are botany, physiology, chemistry and physics. Four terms each must be taken in two of these subjects and two terms in each of the other two, making twelve terms required in the four subjects, that is, twenty-five per cent of the entire University course. Further electives in mineralogy, geology, astronomy and other sciences make possible the presentation of fifty per cent of scientific work. The practical work is broad and comprehensive.

The Home Building.

It is fitting that a word more be said about the farmers' lecture courses. In 1875 a convention of farmers was called at the Agricultural College building and a course attempted; but the farmers did not want it. So the project rested until January, 1882, when a course was inaugurated by the Hon. Geo. B. Loring, United States Commissioner of Agriculture. That was indeed an important day in the history of the Agricultural College. These courses were continued with some of the most eminent men in the country as leaders. Professor Brewer, of Yale and Hon. W. P. Hazard, of Pennsylvania, were perhaps the foremost among them.

The Armory.

The changed conditions of the country as seen when the situation of twenty-five years ago is viewed in the light of present surroundings, suggest that agricultural colleges have for their special function the education of men for schools and colleges of practical agriculture, investigators at experiment stations, experts on dairy and food commissions, and whenever the work assumes a highly technical character. But the development of intelligent, practical, scientific and successful agriculturists is specifically the function of the agricultural school rather than the agricultural college.

The two special features in the development of agricultural education in Minnesota have been: First, the institution of the School of Agriculture; second, the establishment of the Agricultural Experiment Station.

The Agricultural School.

The Agricultural School was opened October 18, 1888. There were enrolled the first year forty-seven students. This school is the outgrowth of much anxious

The Dairy Hall.

deliberation and careful planning on the part of the Regents. The member who gave it at its founding the most careful consideration and brought to the discussion the ripest experience in educational affairs, was D. L. Kiehle, then State Superintendent of Public Instruction. As a member of the Board of Regents he gave direction to the final action of that body. He had in mind a school for farmers' boys in the most explicit meaning of that term. The school was opened with much confidence in the result. That confidence was not misplaced. It has proved to be just the institution the agricultural interests of the state needed. The school has steadily advanced in every element of strength and usefulness since the opening year. In no small degree has the credit for this result been due to the faculty of the school. In 1888 the roster was as follows: Principal, W.W. Pendergast;

Assistant Principal, H. W. Brewster; Teacher of Horticulture and Botany, S. B. Green; Penmanship and Accounts, D.W. Sprague; Animal Breeding,W. M. Hayes; Carpentry and Drawing, C. R. Aldrich; Physiology, Olaf Schwartzkopf. The course of study requires a fair common school education for admission. It extends through three sessions of six months each.

The school has taken on a double function; first, training of expert farmers, and second, preparing for the University course in agriculture. In the eight years of its existence, experience has shown that it offers more practical work than any other Agricultural School in America. All the lines of agricultural work taught cannot be named. One or two can be selected. The art of making butter and cheese is taught by one of the most accomplished experts to be found. Combined with the importance of dairying to the people of the state and the very best facilities for becoming proficient in the art, this work should maintain a foremost place in the School. It also forms a very important feature of the Summer School which has been in operation two seasons.

Dairy Hall.—The Butter Room.

In the fall of 1891 the Dairy School opened with twenty-eight students. In the summer of 1894 the Summer School for ladies gave instruction to fifty-nine students. The enrollment for the first seven years of the School of Agriculture is shown in the following tabulation:

	REGULAR COURSE	DAIRY SCHOOL	SUMMER SCHOOL	COLLEGE COURSE	TOTAL
1888–9	47	......	.....	......	47
1889–90	78	......	....	......	78
1890–1........	104	......	. ....	5	109
1891–2........	88	28	......	3	119
1892–3....	114	30	.....	7	151
1893–4..............	144	59	....	7	210
1894–5.........	204	109	59	9	360

The problem of the education of agricultural communities has been confronted in every state. Throughout the country this School is recognized as the

Minnesota plan. Its success is phenomenal, for it has evolved from the experimental stage into a permanent condition. Committees from other states have come to see its work. England, Germany, Russia, Japan, Canada and Republics of South America, by visits and correspondence, have sought information on the methods employed and the elements of success. Many other states have modeled their schools after it. Out of the number who have attended thus far one only has failed to return to the farm after graduation. We are indeed proud that this department of the University is fulfilling the expectations of those by whom it was established.

On Principal Pendergast's call to the state superintendency of Public Instruction, Dr. Brewster became Principal in charge, which position he has since held. Other changes in the Faculty have occured, some of which can be seen by comparing the above list with that of the present teaching force.

Dairy Hall—The Cheese Room.

In broadening the field of study as time goes on and as the public schools of the state furnish more thoroughly prepared material, the one thing sought for in the maintenance of this school will never knowingly be imperiled. Experience has shown that in spite of a hard and persistent fight the Agricultural College educated its boys and girls away from the farm. The school was founded not only for the farm, but towards the farm. Its history shows that it is most effectually performing that service for the commonwealth.

Student life in the school is made educative and attractive. No pains are spared to surround the young men with every comfort of a home. The rooms of the dormitories are spacious; the facilities for work and exercise sufficient for vigorous health. A large and well-lighted dining hall at stated hours is the busiest department of the school.

The Agricultural Experiment Station.

Before the appropriation by Congress of money for the support of agricultural experimentation in the several states, the Regents organized the State Experiment Station of Minnesota, as directed by law approved March 7, 1885. Dr. Porter was its director.

Pendergast Hall.

The divisions of agriculture, horticulture, entomology, botany, agricultural chemistry and veterinary were established and a specialist was chosen at the head of each division. Since that time dairy husbandry and animal husbandry have been added. The Station has published considerable material relating to the several branches of agricultural science; memoirs and briefer papers have appeared in the Annual Reports of the Station and in the series of forty-four Bulletins thus far issued. In addition, the officers of the Station have prepared much copy for the agricultural press of the state and for the publications of various agricultural and related associations. The Station is an important aid to the School of Agriculture and to every line of agricultural work, both theoretical and applied, carried on by the University. Although only eight years old the Experiment Station has accomplished much good in every line of work it has conducted.

The Gymnasium.

When it shall become fully equipped with men, apparatus and material it will do a far greater work in benefiting the commonwealth than it is doing at present or can point to in the past.

The following lines of work may be mentioned as already opening rich fields of return: Investigations regarding varieties of grains, grasses and other forage plants and their adaptation to Minnesota soil and climate; the adaptation to different sections of the state of vegetables, small fruits, forest and ornamental trees; tests of numerous seedling, small and tree fruits originated in the state and placed under trial by distribution. We can point with pride to the work being done in the way of originating varieties of wheat, oats, barley, corn, timothy, clover and other grains and forage crops for adaptation to Minnesota soils and climate. Many of the ordinary farming operations are being investigated, particularly those which deal with field and garden tillage; the furrow slice and the conservation of moisture around the

The Chemical Laboratory.

roots of growing plants; the management of fields and the rotation of crops. In the line of chemical investigation we commend the work which the Experimental Station has done in the investigation of food stuffs, sugar beets and chemical studies instituted in an extended examination of Minnesota soils. A study has been made of the chemical history of several important agricultural plants; extensive experiments have been performed with live stock. Studies have been made of the cooking of human foods. Every aspect of the dairy industry is receiving careful and scientific attention. The Station has begun extensive lines of research in connection with the diseases of animals; valuable results to the state are already being realized, especially in the practical measures being adopted to lessen the amount

The Veterinary Hospital.

of bovine and indirectly of human tuberculosis. A most complete hospital for the treatment of animal diseases and experimentation upon the same has been provided. Experiments on new plans of medication for horses promise most satisfactory results. In entomology valuable work has been done; we need only mention the restriction upon the ravages of the Rocky Mountain locust and

The Sheep Barn.

chinch bug. The experimental work is constantly increasing in importance. The size of the state and its varied conditions of soil and climate have led the farmers to call for several substations in addition to the central one, the farm. The last Legislature appropriated $20,000 for the establishment of two such stations a n d $10,000 for their support. Such is the record of eight years of active existence.

The College of Law.

The conservative tendency of the governing power of the University is shown in no better way than in the organization of the professional schools of the institution. The College of Law is eminently the outgrowth of the strong public sentiment in the state for such a school. Many inquiries from those wishing to become students in 1887 and preceding years lead the Regents to believe that a law department in the University would meet a real want of the commonwealth; accordingly, in 1888 they voted to establish the department. Honorable William S. Pattee, of Northfield, was elected to the Deanship of the College at the meeting held in March. The history of the school has proved this a most excellent choice. Dean Pattee had since 1874 been a resident of the state; he had won high reputation as teacher in the years during which he was at the head of the Northfield Public Schools. As a lawyer he had guarded the welfare of that city in several legal battles during the years it was his home. His researches into the philosophy and science of law had been the recreation of a busy life. Service in the Legislature had

The Library.

—61—

The Law Building.

Dean Pattee's Office.

accustomed him to parliamentary practice. In the work of instruction a number of the ablest lawyers in the state have been invited to take important lectureships. Courses of lectures from several of these gentlemen have been secured. With a generous regard for the legal education they gave of their ability and experience, and in many instances without compensation. The names of such noted lawyers as Senator S. J. R. McMillan, Hon. Gordon E. Cole, Hon. Chas. D. Kerr, Hon. G. C. Ripley, Hon. James O. Pierce, Hon. Chas. E. Flandreau, Hon. J. M. Shaw and Hon. C. D. O'Brien appear in the first published roster of the faculty of the department.

The department was opened for teaching in September, 1888. There were about thirty students present when Dean Pattee delivered the opening lecture in the old Chapel in University Hall. During that year the number increased to sixty-seven; from that time until the present there has been a rapid and uninterrupted growth, both in the number of students and the efficiency of the College, until there are three hundred and sixty-three students and more than twenty professors, teachers and lecturers. With perhaps one exception, that in New York, there has never been such a rapid development of a law school in this or any other country and it is wholly without parallel if we consider the fact that the institution started *de novo* and not as an offshoot from some other kindred school. From a day school with one course the first year, it has developed through a single course of two years into a day and night

A Lecture Room.

school, each with a course of study extending over three years. In addition to this there is a graduate course of one year; attended only by those who have received the degree of LL. B. from this or some other law school of equal rank.

The graduate courses in law are rapidly becoming a marked feature of the College. The table of attendance given below shows the appreciation of students. It is regarded as the most valuable year in the school by all whose circumstances will permit their attendance. In these courses Minnesota practice, political science, industrial and constitutional law form the more important subjects.

One adjunct of the College which has played no unimportant part in its success is the large and convenient building devoted to its work. It was erected in 1889 and comprises sufficient lecture rooms for the needs of the corps of instructors. This building also contains a good and rapidly growing law library arranged in a large and well lighted reading room. Already several thousand

Laboratory of Medical Sciences

volumes. The generous attitude of the state in ;furnishing publications for exchange has placed the school in a position to command within a few years to come one of the largest working law libraries in the country.

Dean Pattee has devoted himself wholly to the interests of the College. His skill as a teacher, his wise administration and his attractive personality have won the highest success in those broader and more essential fields than mere numbers, either in students or teachers, could have shown.

Further it may be said, and that without any comparison with other most excellent men, that Mr. James Paige has been since 1891 a most faithful and efficient member of the Law Faculty. He has prepared several volumes of cases of a very high order of excellence, which are used with satisfaction in other law schools, and his lectures used in connection with these books are most methodically arranged and clearly stated. His quizzes during the last term of the year are exceedingly searching and helpful.

The following table shows the enrollment in the College of Law since its organization:

	1889	1890	1891	1892	1893	1894	1895	1896
Seniors	4	45	59	78	110	114	117	......
Middle	......	......	......	19	20	26	26	......
Juniors	63	89	117	132	140	145	168	......
Graduate students	......	......	.... .	......	7	25	......	24
TOTALS	67	134	176	229	277	310	334	363

The Department of Medicine.

The original College of Medicine of the University of Minnesota existed in the institution merely as an examining board organized during the year 1883 and discontinued by the Regents in the spring of 1888. It was the outgrowth of a statute providing for a State Board of Medical Examiners and that the provisions of the law should be administered by the Faculty of the University Medical College. It was the duty of the Faculty to test and ascertain by examinations, experiments and other appropriate means the fitness of candidates for the practice of medicine in Minnesota, and to recommend them to the Board of Regents for the appropriate degrees. No instruction was ever given by this College. The idea prevailed that no degrees in medicine should be given by a teaching Faculty who would thereby sit in judgment on their own pupils. The adoption of the present medical law in 1887 relieved the Faculty of duty as an examining board and retirement resulted as soon as the law came into full effect.

Touching the administration of the first Department of Medicine these points may be briefly stated. The first Faculty and State Board of Examiners organized consisted of Dr. Chas. N. Hewitt, Red Wing, Secretary of the State Board of Health, as chairman; and Dr. Perry H. Millard, secretary and executive officer. The other members were Dr. Franklin Staples, of Winona, Professor of the Practice of Medicine; Dr. Daniel W. Hand, of Saint Paul, Professor of Obstetrics and the Diseases of Women and Children; Dr. Chas. E. Smith, of Saint Paul, Professor of Materia Medica and Therapeutics; Dr. George W. Wood, of Faribault, Professor of Diseases of the Nervous System and of Medical Jurisprudence, and Dr. Charles Simpson, of Minneapolis, Professor of Pathology. The degree given was Bachelor of Medicine.

For some years before the institution of a teaching department of Medicine in the University there had been a strong feeling on the part of the physicians in the state that a college of high rank for education in medicine should be opened. The preliminary steps were slowly and carefully taken. Dean Millard had repeatedly urged that the time was ripe, that the auspicious moment had arrived. Yet many things served to delay, as in many an important undertaking, and full fruition was slowly attained. The president immediately upon his arrival in 1884 saw that the field existed for a good teaching school of medicine. He therefore strongly seconded Dean Millard's efforts and with the able assistance of such eminent practitioners as Doctors D. W. Hand, F. A. Dunsmoor, John E. Felton and others, the cornerstone was laid and the superstructure soon appeared.

Medical Hall.

The Department of Medicine thereupon organized embraced:
First, the College of Medicine and Surgery.
Second, the College of Homeopathic Medicine and Surgery.
Third, the College of Dentistry.

The Department of Medicine now in operation differs fundamentally from the college which it displaced in that this is a teaching body; that was an examining board. Instruction was arranged in three distinct courses, one for each of the colleges with a number of the subjects as chemistry, anatomy and other primary branches common to all. Requirements for admission were placed high for that time—only eight years ago—that the profession might be elevated and the hands of the other professional schools throughout the country strengthened. For a time teaching was conducted in the old Medical building in Saint Paul and in the Hospital College building in Minneapolis.

The three colleges above named constituted the entire department until the year 1892, when the College of Pharmacy was added by the Legislature which appropriated $5,000 therefor and directed its establishment.

At the reorganization in the institution of the teaching colleges in 1888, Dr. Millard was made Dean of the department and thus continued so long as the affairs of the colleges were jointly administered. He was assisted by a secretary in each college. The growth of the department and the development of the characteristic features of the respective schools led the authorities to effect a reorganization under which each college was in charge of its respective Dean. This reorganization occured in 1893, and Dean Millard of the department continued as Dean of the College of Medicine and Surgery; Dr. H. W. Brazie was appointed Dean of the College of Homeopathic Medicine and Surgery; Dr. C. M. Bailey, Dean of the College of Dentistry; F. J. Wulling, in 1892 elected Professor of Pharmacy, was at the reorganization in the following year made Dean of the College of Pharmacy. These gentlemen, previous to the reorganization, had served as secretaries of their respective faculties. The only subsequent changes in the heads of the several colleges are these: Dr. A. P. Williamson has been for the past year and is now Dean of the College of Homeopathic Medicine and Surgery, in place of Dean Brazie; Dr. Sudduth who for two years was Dean of the College of Dentistry, resigned in the spring of 1895, and his place was filled by the appointment of Dr. Thomas E. Weeks.

Buildings: The properties originally used for teaching were rented by the Regents for the nominal sum of one dollar per year. The first building of the department upon the Campus, now called Medical Hall, was erected under an appropriation of the legislature in 1891 and occupied in October, 1892. Almost at the same time the smaller building, still in use as a chemical laboratory, was completed and occupied. The former structure cost $65,000 and the latter $6,500. Just occupied at the present writing is a new and beautiful light brick structure, facing Pleasant Street, in the rear of the Chemical and Physical laboratories. This building was erected and equipped for $40,000, appropriated by the legislature of 1895. It marks an epoch in medical education in the state and deserves more than mere mention. It is constructed to meet high scientific demands. It consists of three stories and a high basement, 75 by 150 feet in area. In construction it is slow burning. The east half of the south pavilion is devoted to the College of Pharmacy and is separated from the other compartments by a fire wall. The remainder of the building accommodates (1) the laboratories of histology and embryology, (2) the laboratories of pathology and bacteriology, (3) the laboratories of physiology. A special feature of the basement is a series of capacious cages, aquaria, breeding pens, two large experimental rooms for work in bacteriology and pathology, another for embryology, together with the necessary preparation and store rooms for carrying on the work assigned to the building. The first floor is devoted to histology and contains private laboratories and research rooms for Dr. Lee and the other officers of the department, perfectly lighted students' laboratories, and the necessary lecture rooms. On this floor there are also rooms for the bacteriological work of the State Board of Health, of which board Professor Wesbrook is bacteriologist. The second floor comprises a general laboratory of pathology and bacteriology,

44 by 72 feet, with attached preparation room, office and private laboratory of Dr. Wesbrook; also a demonstration room and a laboratory in physiology. The Ampitheatre extends from this floor to the roof and will accommodate more than two hundred students. On the third floor, so far as it is not taken up by the amphitheatre, are the photographic laboratories and the museum with its several work and preparation rooms. Taking it all in all this building is affirmed to be the most perfect and complete for the uses to which it is devoted to be found in the United States.

The securing of this building makes possible a readjustment of work in the Laboratory Building, under which the chemical laboratories will occupy its entire space. This extension will enable Professor Bell to develop the Department of Chemistry along greatly needed lines of practice and research. The total cost of the buildings to the present time as shown above is not far from $111,500.

Contemporaneous with the inauguration of the four years' courses in the Colleges of Medicine and Surgery and of Homeopathy, the occupancy of the new Laboratory Building means more than the mere addition of facilities for instruction. The development of bacteriology by the appointment of Dr. F. F. Wesbrook, who entered upon his duties in October last, and the lengthening of the time given to this branch; the development of the work in histology, and the emphasis placed upon chemistry and biology as subjects for admission, all point to more exacting and more scientific courses in medicine than have

Medical Chemistry Laboratory.

ever before been required in the western states. Conditions are clearly pointing to the requirement in the near future of a full college course of respectable rank for admission to this vigorous group of colleges.

In speaking of the leading features of the different colleges in this department it is natural to speak first of the College of Medicine and Surgery, since this has in several ways played a leading part in the development of the department. This college aims at no especial and strong features, but rather to be and continue to be a well-balanced organization. That it is such is shown by the fact that over ninety-nine per cent of its students have passed successfully the test of examination. Inasmuch as Michigan shows only ninety-four per cent, the high figure of Minnesota is suggestive.

The College of Homeopathic Medicine and Surgery shows an equally creditable record. The cities of Saint Paul and Minneapolis for a quarter century have

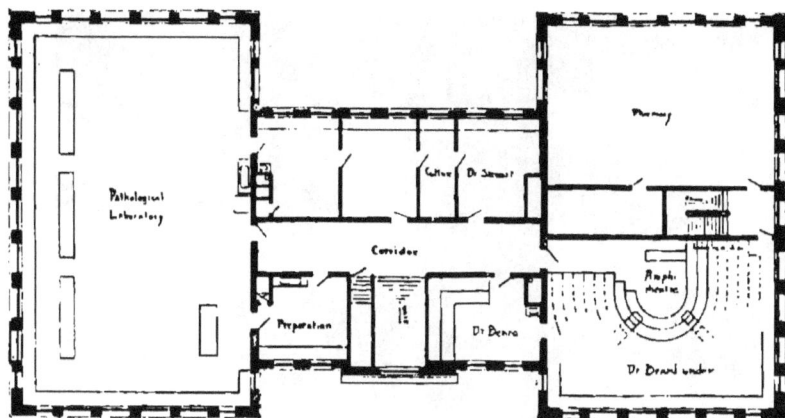

Second Floor Plan

Laboratory of Histology, etc
University of Minnesota
Scale of Feet

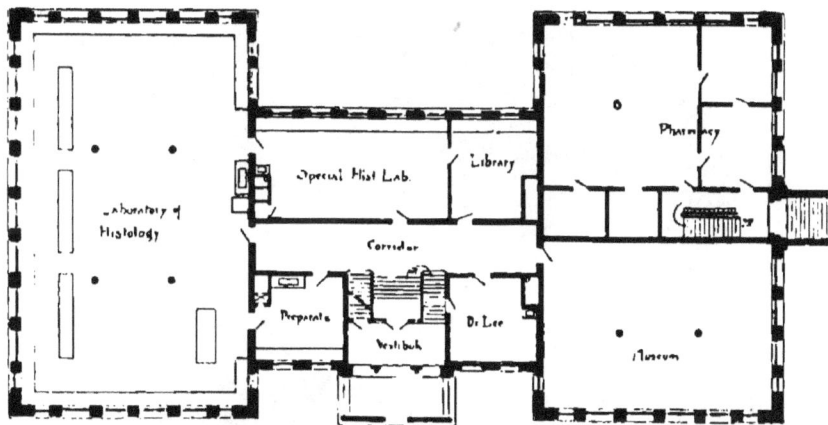

First Floor Plan

Histology—General Laboratory.

Histology and Embryology—General Laboratory.

been a center of homeopathic patronage and interest. Hospitals and clinics offer unrivaled advantages to students for those practical points so essential in the professional education of successful physicians. The gentlemen who occupy the several chairs in this College are enthusiasts; they have won high reputations in their respective specialties and have given to the College a reputation second to none for thoroughness and efficiency.

The seven years' existence of the College of Dentistry has been a period of uninterrupted success and usefulness. The last four years have been passed upon the Campus. The effort of the Faculty from the very outset has been first of all to secure the very best preparation possible in the constituency for entrance upon professional studies, and secondly, to give such thorough scientific training as will make the student ready for the best professional work. The central idea of the institution is that dentistry is a healing art. The ideal has always been high; accordingly, graduate work and original research have been offered and strongly encouraged. It is a matter of pride that no graduate of the college has yet failed to pass the required examination before the State Board of Dental Examiners. The following features of the college are named because they are believed to be unique: The dental branches are taught by manual training and laboratory methods; the instruction from the rostrum is intended only to direct the various operations; members of the Faculty are constantly in attendance in infirmary and laboratory; the scientific and professional laboratories of the whole University are brought into use in perfecting the education of students. By close relationship with the whole University, the broadest university spirit is cultivated.

The College of pharmacy, although the youngest in this group of colleges, is proving a most vigorous associate. The laboratory method is a marked feature of its work. The new building into which the college has but recently moved will give much needed space for the development of this peculiar feature of the college work and soon render it the most conspicuous one. Eight thousand feet of floor space are devoted to it; the basement affording a laboratory for pharmaceutical chemistry and storage; the first floor, the office and space for botany and pharmacognosy; the pharmacological laboratories and prescription department occupy the upper floors.

The various steps that have been taken to advance the standard of the several colleges by requiring higher attainments for admission, longer attendance on lectures and more hours of daily application have never diminished the attendance. It is everywhere recognized that in no department of learning are inferior attainments so dangerous as in medicine. Numbers have uninterruptedly increased from the opening of the department until the present time. With the current year all courses in medicine have been increased to four years. Students, however, coming from accredited colleges may, by submitting satisfactory credits in chemistry and biology, complete their course in three years. The enrollment of the several colleges from the institution of the department to the current year has been as follows:

	1889	1890	1891	1892	1893	1894	1895	1896
Medicine and Surgery..	75	87	124	133	138	169	206	......
Homeo. Med. and Sur..	13	8	15	19	24	17	29	......
Dentistry	22	28	36	39	58	40	64	......
Pharmacy					11	20	26	......
Unclassed students	6	4	15	34	10	38	52	.....
Graduate students							1	
Total students	116	127	190	225	271	284	378	401
Total graduated					58	50	77	....

Pharmacological Laboratory.

Pharmacy—Laboratory Pharmacognosy.

With such a record who can deny that the Medical Department of the University of Minnesota has been one of the most successful ever founded in America and that its future is remarkably bright and hopeful.

❧ ❧ ❧ ❧

The quarter of a century of the University's existence has been one uninterrupted period of rapid expansion in every line of educational activity. Nowhere is this development more apparent than in the general library, to which we all look with especial pride. President Folwell took this line of work under his charge at the very outset and piloted it through the dark days of the University's early history, until today it comprises upwards of 40,000 volumes, carefully selected. Atten-

Laboratory of Medical Chemistry.

tion has been directed in late years toward placing in the General Library such books and periodicals as pertain to the lines of study and research carried on at the institution.

Its present location in the new building makes its facilities for access unexcelled. Students are permitted to handle the books freely and urged to use them as tools in the prosecution of the different phases of intellectual work. Side by side with the General Library are grouped many special libraries of the greatest importance and convenience to those students who are engaged in special lines of investigation. In number and character the publications placed in these libraries are an excellent selection of standard works relating to spe-

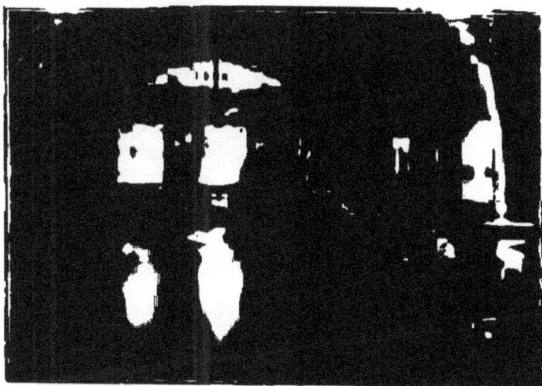

Dentistry—The Operating Room.

cial subjects. The Law Library, that of Medicine, Agriculture, the several lines of Engineering, Botany, Zoology, Geology, Chemistry, Greek and Latin can only be enumerated.

Physiology—Laboratory.

Bacteriology—Culture Room.

Intimately associated with the intellectual life of the University are the numerous literary societies which meet once a week and afford excellent opportunities for practice in extemporaneous speaking and parliamentary procedure, cultivating those qualities which aid in projecting an educated man or woman into the activities of life. From the very first much attention was given to oratory and debating. This has been greatly stimulated through the active interest of Regent Pillsbury, who for some years has annually given three prizes in oratory.

Simultaneous with the department libraries, various societies and journal clubs have been organized for the advancement of learning and general culture among the students in the different departments.

The University, though strictly non-sectarian, is not without the healthful and stimulating influence of numerous religious organizations. These organizations have steadily grown in prosperity and are an important factor in university life. A special feature of their usefulness is in the interest which these organizations take in securing rooms, boarding places and employment for new students as they enter at the beginning of the year.

The social interests of university life are largely centered about the fraternities, which, in all their essential features, are like those of other institutions. Over twenty different fraternities and sororities have an existence here, but by far the larger portion of the student body is still outside of the fraternity circles.

In athletics there has grown up a general interest. The base ball and foot ball teams have won many laurels for the institution, and Field Day is always looked to as one of the interesting events of Commencement week.

Record of Attendance in the Several Lines of Work in the University, 1867-1896.

YEAR	Latin and Prep.	School of Agric.	Artisan & Sum. School	Special All	Academic	Graduates	Professional	Totals	Instructors
1867	72							72	3
1868	109							109	3
1869	213			3	14			230	5
1870	245			12	44			301	9
1871	254			17	50			321	9
1872	204			34	27			265	12
1873	216			15	58			289	13
1874	183			29	75			287	13
1875	131			14	92			247	14
1876	111			36	120			267	14
1877	138			59	143	2		304	18
1878	187			70	114			371	19
1879	190			66	130			386	20
1880	108			41	159			308	17
1881	56		64	38	176	1		271	18
1882	71		93	47	135	9		355	21
1883	53		124	66	104	9		356	28
1884	69		169	57	97	10	2	278	30
1885	54		68	61	110	17		310	29
1886	113		86	50	132	25		411	31
1887	98	14	41	43	194	22		412	33
1888	52	10	113	57	246	21		491	98
1889	40	47	115	87	287	34	177	793	106
1890	46	78	100	101	369	48	260	1002	72
1891		104	74	134	464	45	374	1195	113
1892		129	89	110	503	70	443	1374	119
1893		136	71	218	620	95	490	1680	144
1894		188	192	252	633	121	531	1723	156
1895		281	262	185	762	89	645	2171	165
1896		351	234		1005	137	764	2453	177

Degrees Conferred, 1873-1895.

	1873	1874	1875	1876	1877	1878	1879	1880	1881	1882	1883	1884	1885	1886	1887	1888	1889	1890	1891	1892	1893	1894	1895
B. A.	2	1	3	7	9	5	8	4	10	11	8	9	3	6	7	6	7	10	15	16	26	17	28
B. S.		1	2	5	3	2	10	9	10	9	7	9	3	6	12	12	10	22	14	19	21	36	32
B. L.			1		4	1	6	4	10	11	7	3	6	6	5	14	9	11	17	16	26	19	34
M. A.			1					1	1						1	1	1	1	1	1	4	4	1
M. S.								1		1	2	2	1			1		1		1	1	2	6
M. L.							2					3	2		1	1		9	3	2	2	4	3
Ph. D.			3	3		1					1		1	3	5	2	3	3		4	4	1	7
H. C. E.																					2	1	1
H. N. E.																			2	4	6	2	
B. E. E.																							
B. Min. E.																					1		
B. Met. E.																							
B. Arch.											1		1		1	1							
B. Agr.																						1	2
C. E.																					1	1	
M. E.																						1	
B. F.							2					2		3	2	3							
Min. E.																					1		
LL. B.																3	20	40	49	56	87	89	86
LL. M.																	1				7	14	2
B. Me.																							
M. D.					4											20	17	23	32	45	38	53	
D. D. S.																	6	6	4	13	6	12	
D. Phar.																	7						12
Totals	2	2	9	11	17	15	26	18	28	33	25	29	21	25	32	38	52	119	132	154	248	244	295